W*The*EDDING JOURNEY

A Guide to Your Ceremony,
Personal Vows & Joyful Marriage

REV. HANNAH DESMOND

BALBOA
PRESS
A DIVISION OF HAY HOUSE

Balboa Press books may be ordered through booksellers or by contacting:

Balboa Press
A Division of Hay House
1663 Liberty Drive
Bloomington, IN 47403
www.balboapress.com
1-(877) 407-4847

ISBN: 978-1-4525-3993-5 (sc)
ISBN: 978-1-4525-3994-2 (hc)
ISBN: 978-1-4525-3992-8 (e)

Library of Congress Control Number: 2011917692

Because of the dynamic nature of the Internet, any web addresses or links contained in this book may have changed since publication and may no longer be valid. The views expressed in this work are solely those of the author and do not necessarily reflect the views of the publisher, and the publisher hereby disclaims any responsibility for them.

The author of this book does not dispense medical advice or prescribe the use of any technique as a form of treatment for physical, emotional, or medical problems without the advice of a physician, either directly or indirectly. The intent of the author is only to offer information of a general nature to help you in your quest for emotional and spiritual well-being. In the event you use any of the information in this book for yourself, which is your constitutional right, the author and the publisher assume no responsibility for your actions.

Any people depicted in stock imagery provided by Thinkstock are models, and such images are being used for illustrative purposes only.
Certain stock imagery © Thinkstock.

Printed in the United States of America

Balboa Press rev. date: 12/15/2011

In Gratitude

With Gratitude to all of the couples I have married through the years. Being part of the happiest day of your lives was a great privilege.

Thanks to my husband, Tom, who believes in me and supports all of my endeavors.

Thanks to Lois Clement for sharing her computer wisdom.

Thanks to Elaine Kolp for her assistance with the astrological portion of this book.

Love and gratitude to Shauna Mathis for her clear vision and kind words.

Contents

Introduction

The opening of the heart to love is an experience we all long for. When you experience the joy of giving and receiving unconditional love and acceptance with that one special person, your thoughts turn to commitment and marriage. As you begin to plan the wedding you also begin to search for the words to honor and express the feelings you have for your relationship. For some the words flow easily, for many there seem to be no words to express their joy. The information in this book assists couples in expressing, in a variety of ways, their feelings of love and commitment and provides methods of accessing the deeper emotions they wish to express.

When my husband and I began to create our wedding ceremony thirty five years ago, we knew we did not want a traditional wedding but we were not sure what form our ceremony would take. Together, we worked on creating a ceremony that would reflect our authentic selves, our life philosophy and, most importantly, our love for one another. Those weeks of sharing and exploring our hearts together were one of the most meaningful times in our relationship. The deep conversation and phrasing of our vows deepened our relationship and our appreciation of one another.

Working with couples and assisting in the creation of wedding ceremonies for twenty years, I have seen many couple who wish to have a unique ceremony that truly expresses their love, beliefs and the vision they hold for their life together. Couples often want to create personal vows in a light hearted, poetic or deeply personal way. There are those who easily express their feelings and those who struggle to express their heartfelt emotions. I have included within this book information, techniques and tips to assist you in creating your personal wedding vows and wedding scripts to inspire your ceremony.

The components of the ceremony are explained, both the traditional unfolding of the wedding itself, and the meaning of the different parts. As you understand the purpose of each part of the ceremony, you are prepared to change, omit, add to, or reconfigure your wedding to reflect your beliefs, life philosophy and loving commitment to one another

Each wedding script serves as a template you can work with to create something that is uniquely yours. You may want to use parts from several scripts. Read the ceremonies with your fiancé; feel which parts resonate with you and create the wedding that genuinely expresses your bond of love. The "Intention" section of each ceremony can serve as an inspiration for your own personal vows.

Included in the wedding ceremony section is information on the Celtic ritual of Handfasting. This ancient rite is enjoying a new popularity in the modern weddings of today. Handfasting is a ritual that can be incorporated within a wedding or used alone. This ancient ceremony is where the term "tying the knot" originated.

A variety of unity rituals are described following the wedding scripts. From the lighting of a candle together to the gifting of gemstones to the combining of wines, there are rituals which symbolize your union and can include family members and friends.

The wedding ceremonies, vows, blessings and unity rituals within this book serve as guides. You may choose to add favorite quotes, personal expressions of love and your life philosophy. Keep in mind, this is your ceremony and the words you speak reflect who you are, your relationship and your intentions for the future.

You will also find information on the wisdom of having an astrological wedding chart created. The wedding chart combines the birth chart of the bride and groom bringing a greater understanding of the cosmology of your relationship and the energies you both bring into the marriage. The gemstones, colors, flowers and metals that are assigned to each astrological sign are included. This information is a fun and symbolic way to join the energy of the bride and groom together throughout the wedding ceremony and reception.

Today many men and women are entering same sex marriages. At this time, not all states recognize these marriages as legal; however, the ceremony and the loving commitment expressed create a marriage. With this truth in mind, the ceremonies within this book can easily be modified and used as commitment ceremonies.

Information and practices to assist the bride and groom in the relief of stress and anxiety as they plan their wedding are offered as well as tools for exploring pathways to self-awareness and heart centered living. In marriage, the more self-aware you become, the more love and acceptance you can share with your partner. An emotional response scale provides examples of how to move from anxiety, fear, and frustration into more soothed emotional states. This is a tool that will be beneficial throughout your life. Opening to self-knowledge and inner balance allows a more deeply conscious union and the experience of great happiness and soul connection within a lasting marriage. Because this awareness is so important in maintaining, nurturing and expanding your love and connection in relationship, it is vital information for those contemplating marriage.

This book is written with the sincere wish that it be of assistance through the planning of a joyful ceremony, a heart centered wedding and a marriage of loving co-creation, mutual respect and great love.

welchphotovideo.com

PART I

THE COMPONENTS OF THE CEREMONY

The Components of the Ceremony

Your wedding is the foundation of your marriage. The most important component of the ceremony is the exchange of your marriage vows. The second most important part is the decree of marriage by the celebrant, making the sacred union legal. The rest of the ceremony provides an opportunity for the creative expression of your love for one another, the statement of your intentions for your life together, gratitude to family and friends, spiritual blessings, poetry, music and cultural traditions.

The Processional

The ceremony begins after the seating of the bride's mother. The wedding celebrant, followed by the groom, walk down the aisle and take their places. The bridesmaids, ring bearer and flower girl precede the bride down the aisle.

The ritual begins with the bride and groom apart from one another. The groom stands waiting at the altar and the bride appears at the other end of the aisle. The bride approaches her groom and the separate lives of the two individuals begin the transformation into the oneness of marriage. Friends and relatives stand for the processional to honor the beginning of this sacred transformation.

The Convocation

The convocation is a short statement which begins the ritual. It is at this time the celebrant invites the family and friends attending to witness the ceremony and add their positive intentions and loving support to the couple.

The Invocation

During the invocation the celebrant will call upon the energy which guides you in your life. If you are having a traditional Christian wedding, God or Jesus may be invoked. In Spiritual weddings the celebrant may call upon Universal Energy, Your Higher Selves or the Energy of Love.

The Address

The celebrant will speak for a few minutes about marriage.

If there is to be a poem, reading, personal story or song, the celebrant can introduce this portion after the address.

The Consecration

The consecration introduces a deeper sense of the sacredness of the vows which are about to be exchanged. At this time reminders of the joys of true commitment and the sharing of a life filled with understanding, unconditional love and acceptance may be stated.

The Exchange of Vows

The exchange of vows is the heart of the wedding ceremony. The vows are equally powerful whether they are spoken from the heart, read or repeated. You may choose to create your own vows or have your celebrant assist you in selecting or creating vows that express your love and commitment.

The Exchange of Rings

The celebrant will ask for the rings and the best man will place the two rings in her hand. She then offers words or a blessing, as she holds the rings. The groom will be given the brides ring and he may speak words of his own creation or repeat words that have been previously chosen as he places the ring on her finger. The bride then places the grooms ring on his finger.

The Proclamation

The exchange of rings is followed by the announcement of marriage by the celebrant, the kiss and the presentation of the bride and groom as a married couple.

The couple walks down the aisle together followed by the wedding party, the bride's parents, the grooms' parents and the minister.

Helpful Suggestions for Your Wedding Day

The Wedding Party:

As you begin to put together your wedding party, choose friends and family members who are meaningful in your life. Close friends or relatives will happily assist you in the weeks leading up to the wedding and stand with you as you make your vows on your wedding day.

This is not the time to fulfill obligations but the time to have those who are dearest to you close by your side. These are the people who witness and remember the vows you speak and the commitment made during your ceremony. Through the years they will be a part of your life and support your relationship.

The bridesmaids do not have to be young and beautiful. You may choose to have an older neighbor who you have known and loved for years stand with you, knowing her love and support has been steady and true through the years. You may have a male friend stand with you or a young girl as a junior bridesmaid.

The groom, also, will want to have his closest friends standing with him. Both the bridesmaids and groomsmen play an important part in the weeks leading up to the ceremony. If you do not have a wedding planner, your attendants assist in the running of errands, fielding phone calls and putting together your wedding day emergency kit. This kit contains items like safety pins, an extra pair of hose, deodorant, perfume, hairspray and anything else you may need to have at hand directly before the wedding. Be sure that one of your attendants brings a snack for you. Crackers, a container of yogurt or fruit and cheese to settle a jittery stomach. It is important that you eat the day of the wedding. Keeping your blood sugar regulated assists in keeping your mind clear and your nervous system calm. As you dress for the wedding ceremony, your maid of honor and best man will be assisting you. During the marriage ceremony, they will hold your bouquet, arrange the train of your dress, hold the wedding rings, hand you a handkerchief and provide any other functions you include in your service. Choose those individuals who love you and will be supportive. Remember to show your gratitude and love for all the help by gifting them with a keepsake.

Children in the Wedding Party

After attending hundreds of weddings, it is my observation that the children involved in the wedding party perform beautifully, enjoy participating and retain beautiful memories of their part in the wedding if they are at least four years old. Children younger than four are generally either terrified or unaware of what is expected of them. Small children, screaming in terror directly before the bride walks down the aisle, will change the tone you have created for your ceremony. I have seen smaller children put in a decorated wagon and pulled down the aisle then seated with relatives whom they know and love. This is a good way to make the younger members of the family feel special without causing them anxiety.

If you would like to include more family members than just the flower girl and ring bearer, there are several fun roles children over four years old can fill. You may want to include a child waving small flags or pendants made of beautiful paper or fabric matching the wedding colors. Another child may carry a bell resting on a pillow. The bell can be rung at the end of the service when you kiss. A little girl may enjoy waving a magic wand as she walks down the aisle, proud to be part of the wedding party. An older child may carry an incense holder, filling the air with sacred scent. The children can sit on cushions in front of the bridesmaids and groomsmen.

Dogs in the Wedding Party:

The family dog is often included in the wedding party. Making sure that an adult has the dog on a leash and is in charge of removing him from the scene if the unexpected happens, is a good idea.

The Celebrant:

Choose a celebrant who you feel comfortable with. This is a person who understands and is part of the spirit you wish to create at your ceremony. If you are planning on creating your own vows, be sure to discuss this with the celebrant before you hire him/her to perform your service. It is a good idea to meet with the celebrant before the rehearsal or wedding day. This way you will be able to assess your compatibility, hear the sound of his/her voice and discuss the color scheme for your wedding, assuring their choice of attire for the wedding will blend with the colors you have chosen.

The celebrant for your ceremony, whether it is a minister, judge, justice of the peace or priest, is a member of your wedding party. If the celebrant attends the rehearsal he/she is also invited to the rehearsal dinner. Remember to also invite him/her to stay for the wedding reception.

Talk to your celebrant about how and when he/she would like to receive payment for the service. Traditionally the celebrant is paid at the rehearsal or at the signing of the marriage license. You may put a parent or the wedding planner in charge of making sure the celebrant is paid.

If your celebrant has another engagement soon after your ceremony, you can arrange to sign the marriage license immediately after the service or before the ceremony.

Outdoor Summer Weddings

For those who choose to have an outdoor summer wedding, it is best to plan the wedding for late afternoon or early evening. Provide a hand held fan on the seat of each guests' chair. Make sure there are large fans keeping the air moving if the wedding is in an outdoor pavilion. I have been to a number of summer weddings in places that are not usually too warm. Unfortunately, the day of the wedding a heat wave sweeps through and everyone is melting.

Consider your comfort as you select your attire and the attire for the bridesmaids and groomsmen. Consider the comfort of your guests and try to seat them in the shade.

Outdoor Spring and Fall Weddings

The weather is often beautiful during the Spring and Fall months, but unexpected cool or rainy weather can surprise those who have planned an outdoor event. In the Spring and Fall renting a tent in case of rain showers will relieve a lot of needless concern on your wedding day. An open sided tent is usually all that is needed. If the weather forecast suddenly calls for chilly winds, an enclosed tent with heaters will assure you, your wedding party and your guests will be comfortable. These suggestions may seem obvious, however, I have seen many shivering brides, bridesmaids and guests. An outdoor ceremony, taking advantage of the beauty of nature, is a dream for many brides and grooms. Spending the entire ceremony freezing, shivering and watching your bridesmaids turn blue puts a damper on the beauty of nature and the joy of the day.

Another good idea is to have an optional wrap, shawl or small jacket that the bride and bridesmaids can wear if the weather is too cool for the strapless or sleeveless gowns they are planning to wear.

If an indoor option is available, I advise you move the wedding inside so you can be totally present both physically and emotionally.

When the Ceremony is Delayed

It happens occasionally that a ceremony has to be delayed, sometimes for several hours. Situations with flight arrivals, cars breaking down, chartered buses stuck in traffic can have a devastating effect on a wedding. The best thing to do is make the guests, who have arrived on time, comfortable. Open the bar, serve hor's dourves and allow them to be seated. If the musicians have arrived you may ask them to begin playing assuring them their payment will be increased.

The Wedding Veil:

Long bridal veils are beautiful. However, if you are having an outdoor wedding where you will be walking over grass, gravel, cement or plywood, as in the flooring of the outdoor tent, a long veil easily catches. I have seen numerous brides serenely walking down the aisle at their outdoor venues stop suddenly, grab their head piece as the veil is tugged, sometimes coming off entirely as it drags on the ground. Consider a shorter veil for outdoor ceremonies.

Personal Vows:

The personal vows the bride and groom have written for the ceremony can be entrusted to the best man to hold in his suit jacket pocket. At the appropriate time he can give them to the wedding celebrant who will hand them to the bride and groom. If there are no attendants, a friend or family member may hold them and bring them up at the appointed time or they may be placed on a small table nearby. The celebrant may also hold them and hand them to the bride and groom. Most brides and grooms do not memorize their personal vows. The celebrant does not usually speak the personal vows and ask the couple to repeat them.

Immediately After the Ceremony:

Allow a little time for the newlyweds to share a few quiet moments together. They can hold one another, allow the joy of their new union to be felt and expressed. The processing of the ritual and the vows they have made to one another begins in these first moments. The signing of the marriage license follows. Photos can wait or group pictures of the wedding party can be started as the bride and groom share a few moments with one another and sign their marriage license.

Your Wedding Day, Your Way

A wedding is a day celebrating love. While those who are invited to a wedding look forward to the positive experience of affirming love, having fun and enjoying community, those who are planning a wedding can experience stress and anxiety as they plan this momentous occasion. I encourage the bride, groom and their parents to take a deep breath and relax. Within this book there are several relaxation techniques that are very useful during the planning of the wedding. Read through them and practice those that work for you. Allow the planning of the wedding to be a joyful, heartwarming, positive experience.

The most important part of your wedding day is the vows you speak to one another during your ceremony. I encourage you to be an active participant in creating the ceremony as the love and commitment expressed through your vows are written in your hearts. While not all couples want to write their own personal vows, having input into the creation of the vows, the ring blessing and the words spoken as rings are exchanged, assures that your true sentiments, beliefs and your devotion to one another is expressed and heard with all of your being.

As the bride and groom begin to create their ceremony the questions are: "what have you always dreamed your wedding ceremony would be like?" "What components do you want to include?" "Do you have a certain song, poem or cultural tradition you want to include?" "What words or sentiments have you dreamed of expressing to your beloved?" Incorporating your authentic selves and expressing your love in your own words creates a ceremony that is powerful, deeply meaningful and memorable.

I have attended hundreds of weddings and enjoyed them all. There are weddings planned for months by professionals with everything coordinated and there are weddings put together in two weeks, with no rehearsal. There are those who elope to a city they have never visited and those who have the ceremony in the family garden. Some weddings serve champagne; some have a keg of beer. No matter what your budget, no matter where you are having your wedding, the key ingredient is loving relaxation. As the Beatles said, "Let it be" enjoy the event as it unfolds and embrace the day, savoring every minute. The minutes add up to memories you will enjoy and share with your children and grandchildren.

Traditional weddings are beautiful, but which traditions have meaning to you? Create your wedding filled with the people, words, song and rituals that are meaningful to you. Kudos to those couples who have their beloved dog serve as their flower girl, to the couple who had the bride's twin sisters perform a short ballet number during the ceremony, to the couples who get married barefooted, to the bride who grabs her guitar and sings her personal vows. I encourage couples to be themselves, express themselves and create the ceremony that reflects their love, their uniqueness and their joy. Let your wedding be truly YOUR wedding.

Every couple wants their wedding to go smoothly. You will remember your wedding day forever and don't want to have disasters be part of your memories. While I haven't witnessed any disastrous weddings, I have seen a few that had some funny kinks. It is when the unexpected happens that the emotional preparation the bride and groom have done before the wedding is truly valuable. I encourage you to use the relaxations and guided mediations within this book to help you center yourself and enjoy serenity throughout the wedding and the reception.

I remember one country wedding which was held in a small gazebo next to a babbling brook. The setting was beautiful, the groom and his groomsmen, in their tuxedos, awaited the arrival of the bride and her attendants. Time ticked by and the bride did not arrive. A phone call confirmed that the limo to bring her down the country road and deliver her to the gazebo did not arrive. Several minutes later as the musicians were playing softly; a pick-up truck came tearing across the field, bride and her attendants bouncing in the back of the pick-up. The driver pulled up beneath the trees and the bride and her bridesmaids daintily descends out the back of the truck. As the bridesmaids made their way up the aisle, the bride's dad walked over, she took his arm and with a big smile on her face, the bride walked toward her groom, who had tears of joy in his eyes.

Today dogs are more a part of the family than ever before. Many people consider them to be almost like children. I love seeing dogs participating in the wedding, if they are well trained and have someone to handle them beside the bride or groom.

Cruise, a blond lab and long-time member of the family, was the ring bearer at a beautiful medieval themed wedding. The dog had the wedding rings in a small bag, tied to his collar. The outdoor path down to the wedding site was long and Cruise got distracted, broke free from the young bridesmaid who had his leash, and proceeded to run off with the rings. It took 15 minutes to catch up with him and caused some stress to the bride and groom and a good bit of laughter among the guests. It was then that I decided that dogs make better flower girls than ring bearers.

Mr. Pete, a wire haired terrier, looked very distinguished, wearing a red bow tie that matched those of the other groomsmen. He was listed in the program as one of the groomsmen. Unfortunately, Mr. Pete, grew a bit antsy during the wedding, lifted his leg and relieved himself all over the best mans' shoes.

Even though these things were not in the plan for the wedding, they did make for great stories the bride and groom could share for years.

Feel free to create your event with dogs, birds, butterflies, accordions, bongo drums, bagpipes and anything else that makes you feel happy and creates an authentic reflection of you and your partner. Wear a red dress, a kilt, a big green hat or whatever makes you feel beautiful.

I loved the groom who wore red high tops with his tuxedo, the bride and bridesmaids who roller skated around the fountain and up the long aisle at their outside venue.

There was one couple who had met at a small park next to a river. They planned their wedding to take place in the exact spot where they met exactly one year before. The day of the wedding dawned cloudy with a light drizzle. Arriving at the park, I suggested we hold the ceremony in the picturesque gazebo. The bride and groom nixed the idea and the ceremony was held in the spot where they had met, now the site of a deluge. I was thankful one of the groomsmen held an umbrella over me. The bride and groom got drenched but the wedding kiss was the best one I've ever witnessed.

Even when the unexpected happens, enjoy it. It is all a part of the story of your wedding day. Let nothing distract you from the purpose of professing your love and experiencing the joy of your union.

A Deeper Look: Heart Centered Living And Your Wedding Vows

As we move into the new paradigm of thought in the 21st century, the way we live and think is shifting to an awareness and responsibility for the thoughts and words we incorporate in the creation of our lives. This same awareness is an important factor in the ongoing co-creative work of marriage. Recognizing the emotions that arise from your heart as you think different thoughts, use different words and give attention to the actions that follow brings awareness of your active participation in the creation of every situation in your life. This paradigm is called, heart centered living.

Being mindful of heart centered living and co-creation through positive thought advances the structure of the wedding ceremony into a compelling expression of the life you are creating together. In this new awareness, wedding vows encompass and embrace the allowing, acceptance and sharing of expansions in consciousness, compassion, spirituality and wisdom through time.

The exchange of vows is the heart of the wedding ceremony. The words you speak to one another on your wedding day are the expression of your deepest feelings. When you are speaking from your heart, your true voice is accessed. Your true voice carries creative potential which gives energy to your beliefs, and the dreams and visions you intend to manifest in your life together. It is here that the conscious use of words and the emotions they evoke is vitally important.

Great love and deep commitment are every couple's intention as they make their vows to one another. Words of fear, struggle, sickness and other difficulties need not be included in the marriage ceremony. By expressing the things that are not wanted such as illness and poverty, they can become an unwelcomed part of the matrix of energy created during the ceremony. A simple statement such as, "to love one another through all that life may bring" is a good way to acknowledge that whatever challenges arise, they will be met together. Let your wedding vows state that as you meet challenges, your thoughts will be of solutions, your words will be encouraging and, together, you will hold a vision of positive outcome.

The vows are the heart of the ceremony and the rings are the symbols of the love and commitment shared. They are the outward symbol of the inner marriage, the visible sign you bring away from the wedding ceremony. The words spoken during the exchange of rings are a magical binding filled with love and promise. As the celebrant offers a blessing over the rings, the words she speaks set the tone for the words you will share as you place the ring on the second finger of the left hand. The energy of this finger is believed to lead directly to the heart. The precious metals and gemstones used in the rings energize the heart connection, strengthening the bonds of love and commitment.

Work with one another and your celebrant to create a ceremony that truly reflects the truth of who you are and the love you share. Parents or grandparents sometimes want to hear a certain prayer or quote in the service. If you are comfortable with their choice, it is a beautiful way to acknowledge your love and acceptance of them. If you are not comfortable, you may ask your celebrant to suggest a prayer or quote that would resonate more with all of you. As you walk down the aisle together, newly wedded, your hearts will be filled with love, joy and gratitude for one another and all those who assisted in the creation of your beautiful ceremony.

Tips For Creating Your
Personal Vows

No one can tell you exactly how to write your vows, as they must come from your heart. Here is an offering of suggestions, words and phrases to help you begin the process.

- ♥ Before you begin to write your vows, go within and allow your emotions to guide you. The feelings that arise, the statements that ring true within your heart are the essence of the vows you are making to one another.
- ♥ The most important ingredient in your personal vows is your authentic voice. Speak to one another as if you were alone, for indeed, in that moment time stands still and you are in sacred space where no other can distract you or judge your words.
- ♥ Your vows do not have to be long, witty or poetic. You may want to speak about the first moment you saw her or him. Celebrate the love that has grown between you and state your intention as a husband or wife.
- ♥ It is okay to write your vows together and share them one another as you plan your wedding ceremony or write them separately and read them to one another for the first time during your ceremony.

♥ Words such as loving trust, appreciation, respect, cherish, support and encouragement may be used to express your feelings and the promises you wish to make. The idea of sharing dreams and building a life together, offering strength and comfort, respect and laughter are wonderful sentiments to include.

♥ Promises to grow with one another in mind and spirit, to be open, honest and faithful are often included.

♥ The vows can end with a statement such as "I am overjoyed to be marrying you and thank you for becoming my wife/husband." "I give you my hand, my heart and my love forever."

WORKSHEET FOR THE BRIDES PERSONAL VOWS

You may use this page to write any thoughts, ideas or visions that come to you as you close your eyes and imagine speaking your vows on your wedding day. This is where you write whatever comes to mind. There is no form or structure, no right or wrong way or idea. Let your intellect go and let your heart express itself. There is time later to come back and glean the essence of what you wrote, creating vows from your heart.

WORKSHEET FOR THE GROOMS PERSONAL VOWS

This page is to assist the groom in the creation of his personal vows. First, read through the previous chapters, A Deeper Look: Heart Centered Living and Your Wedding Vows and Tips for Creating Your Personal Vows. Without consulting your intellect begin to write. Allow the heart to express itself. Do not judge what you write. Allow your emotions to flow onto the page. There is no right or wrong sentiment, expression or word. Later, return to this page and use your heartfelt expressions as you create your personal vows.

The Bride's Preparation

The day of the wedding has arrived and the ceremony has begun. The bride receives a kiss of farewell from her father and steps up to take her place next to her groom. Holding her bouquet of flowers, symbolizing beauty, fertility and perfection, the bride embodies the archetype of the goddess, sacred receptive energy.

The groom watches his bride approach, often with tears of joy in his eyes. As the archetype of the protector, he stands tall and welcomes her to stand beside him on his left side, near to his heart. As they stand together in sacred space, the ritual begins.

Every bride dreams of this moment during the planning of her wedding. The months and weeks leading up to the ceremony are filled with tasks, parties, planning and shopping. It is important to take time, throughout the hectic planning to stay in touch with your feelings. For the most part, the feelings that arise are joyful. But you could also have a sense of anxiety about the logistics of this important event you are planning. Deeper emotions may surface with this very significant change in your life.

It is important that emotions are allowed to arise, not only the feeling of joy but also any anxiety, fear and confusion you may be feeling. It is natural for tears to come as you realize that your relationship with your mother, father and your girlfriends will change once you are married. These relationships are not ending but there will be changes as your priorities shift to your married life. Unsettling emotions are a normal part of the transformational process of marriage.

The truth about painful emotions is that they have to be acknowledged. Pushing the emotions aside, distracting yourself with another task assures that the emotions will manifest in some other way. This energy can show up as anything from *bridezilla* behavior, sobbing and red puffy eyes on your wedding day to a pimple on your chin.

Science has proven that energy cannot be destroyed but it can be transformed. Unsettling emotions are the result of thought energy and painful emotional energy trapped in the body. The best way to begin the transformation of unsettling emotions such as fear, anxiety and nervousness is to recognize what they are and transform them into energy that can serve your highest good.

Visualization For Transforming Negative Emotions Into Soothing Emotions

For personal peace and personal growth take a moment to acknowledge whatever fear, anger, confusion or other painful emotion you may be experiencing. The cause of your unsettling emotion does not have to be figured out or dwelled upon. Sit quietly, breathe and allow yourself to feel the emotion. Pass no judgment. Feel how acknowledging this emotion impacts your body and your nervous system. Make the intention to transform this energy into positive energy that can serve your highest good. This is not wishing it away but intention followed by transformative action. Following the instructions here will assist in the intentional transformation; using your breath and your awareness

- Notice first that the feeling has a physical presence like a black cloud or an ache in a particular part of your body. Take a deep breath and as you exhale, visualize the black cloud lighting to grey. Notice the ache in your body responding as it eases a bit.

- Another deep breath with the intention of transforming the emotion, on the exhale, the grey cloud changes to blue.
- With every inhale and exhale the cloud lightens, moving from blue, to sky blue from sky blue to violet. With every inhale and exhale the physical ache in the body relaxes and releases a little more.
- With every intentional breath you are transforming the energy. Allow the cloud to move from violet to soft pink.
- Once the cloud is pink, breathe it into your heart. Stretch your body and notice the stiffness and ache have dispersed.
- You have begun the process of accepting and transforming emotions that cause you pain and allowing yourself to be calmed. The simple act of stillness, silence and focusing on the breath is a powerful tool to self-awareness and transformation.
- Using these soothing feelings begin to think thoughts that support you. Visualize and intend a wedding day where you are composed, receptive, totally present and blissful.
- Notice the feelings that accompany these thoughts. Thoughts and feelings are powerful. They are the building blocks of your reality. Use them to create the wedding and the life you want.
- As you think each thought, follow the emotion that arises. If your thoughts begin to lead you into fear and anxiety gently move to a thought that is more soothing, visualize breathing the pink energy into your heart as it leads you away from negativity and into serenity. Living

from a place of serenity is a gift you give yourself and all those who interact with you.

This simple breathing visualization and thought awareness exercise can be used throughout your life whenever you feel the need. Teach this to your husband and friends so they, too, can enjoy the positive results.

You can choose to create a wedding day filled with calamities in your mind, or you can pre-pave a day of sacredness and celebration where all runs smoothly. The thoughts you think and the emotional energy you embody have a strong impact on the flow of your life. If thinking of horrible Uncle Harold getting drunk at your wedding brings you distress, think of his wife keeping an eye on him and steering him away from the open bar.

Loving, satisfying thoughts are sometimes difficult to entertain. When you find yourself unable to move into happy, move into the next best feeling you can. You can refer to the Emotional Response Guide in the final section of this book to assist you in following your emotional tones. Forcing yourself into a false sense of joy is not going to have the same long term effect that taking time to gently move yourself up the scale of emotions into a better feeling place will. Remember emotions are thoughts moving through your body. By breathing and taking the time to shift your thoughts in a more positive, uplifting direction, the anxiety in the body dissipates as the emotions moving through you are now more soothing. Practicing these transformative exercises will serve you throughout your life. It may seem difficult at first, but the more you practice the more easily you will embody calmness, presence and peace. It is a good practice to journal about your experiences during the planning of your wedding. Include your feelings of joy, love and anticipation and your experiences of transforming the negative thoughts and feelings into energy that serves you. This journal can be a wonderful gift to your own daughter or granddaughter as she plans her wedding.

♥ Talk with parents, friends, your fiancé, a therapist or your wedding celebrant about the emotions and changes you are experiencing. Sharing your concerns and receiving assurance of unconditional love and support builds bridges of trust, mutual support, deep friendship and love.

♥ Take time for yourself, putting your attention on the natural pattern of your inhale and exhale quiets the minds' inner chatter, what is sometimes called the monkey mind. This simple technique connects you to your inner being where wisdom and peace reside.

♥ Walk in nature, enjoy a mountain hike, a stroll along the beach or rivers shore. Allow the easy spirit of nature to soothe you. Walking stills the mind and assists the body in releasing blocked energy.

♥ At home you can sit quietly and listen to soothing music. Choosing music that has no emotional charge, for you, allows the mind and body to relax.

♥ Moving your body through the practice of yoga, Qui gong, Thai Chi or dance helps break up stagnant energy in the body and transform it to available energy for the planning of your wedding.

♥ Taking time to listen to guided meditations filled with suggestions for deep relaxation is a wonderful and effective way to calm inner turmoil and attain a state of peaceful anticipation rather than anxiety around your wedding day.

These calming exercises allow the mind to become still and the nervous system to relax. It is through time spent with yourself, contacting your inner being that you begin to know your true inner self. Being self—aware brings a sense of confidence. Self—confidence assists you in moving through the changes coming in your life, for letting go of the old reality and stepping into your future as a married woman. Doing the emotional work necessary brings a sense of clarity, acceptance, and receptiveness to the transitions that are part of the wedding ceremony. Taking time to let go of fear and anxiety and focusing on the intended life you want to create with your husband assists in tapping into your own power and brings a positive focus on your new life.

Your wedding is a rite of passage from the life of a single woman to the life of a married woman. Knowing that you want to be married and accepting that changes are part of your personal and spiritual evolution prepares you to enter the ceremony with a clear head and heart, embracing the day in joy and peace.

WORKSHEET FOR THE BRIDES PREPARATION

After you practice the exercises for relaxation, awareness and transformation in The Bride's Preparation chapter, take time to write any emotions, ideas, dreams, visions and thoughts that occurred. These insights and realizations are signposts to your path of personal evolution and assist you as you become part of a loving, committed partnership.

whiteboxweddings.com

For the Groom

In many cases it is the bride who is the driving force behind the wedding planning. It is "her day." The groom goes along with all the plans and decisions and tries to be a good sport. It is a testament to his love for bride when he diplomatically gives his opinion of the table decorations or the bride's maid's dresses.

While the planning for the wedding occupies the bride, the groom has time to go within and contemplate his role as a husband. I would venture to say that there are not a lot of grooms that take this time for introspection.

Men, by nature, are active, they see a problem, sense a need and they are immediately motivated to fix things. This is wonderful when it is something that can be fixed with a wrench. Emotions, within themselves and in their beloved do not need to be fixed. As a new husband or supportive fiancé, you can "fix" your beloved's crying bout or anxiety with listening. Often open arms and open ears are the best solution. Emotions within yourself can be recognized and released using the techniques discussed throughout this book; the use of the breath, the conscious choosing of better thoughts, time spent in nature, activity to release stress from the physical body, and the expression of the emotions to a friend or by journaling.

Here are a few simple techniques that you can incorporate into your life which will bring you to a more relaxed and open state of love and awareness. These techniques strengthen your marriage and create a lifetime of mutual love and support.

Allowing time for being alone in quietness offers a space for the recognition of emotions. As you begin this introspective state thoughts may race through your head, thoughts of things you must do, want to do, think you need to do. Acknowledge that these are thoughts and you will deal with them later. Let thoughts of outer activities go and allow yourself to feel your emotions. Recognizing your emotions and allowing them to arise within you is healing. Breathing into the emotions and into tightness or tension in the body is an excellent way to come to a state of balance and acceptance of your own inner processes. Experiencing fears and doubts is natural. It does not mean you are marrying the wrong person. These are normal emotions that arise as you move toward a day of commitment to another.

During the courting period of the relationship you spend a lot of time with your fiancée doing things together. Once you are married it is important to take time for activities and also time for the simple act of "being" developing the ability to spend time in comfortable silence with one another and allow an awareness of your thoughts, the energy that follows the thoughts and tension in the body. Being with your mate in comfortable silence allows you to "tune in" to your subtle energy thereby getting to know yourself better and also becoming aware of your mates subtle energies.

New awareness of self—love, forgiveness, self—acceptance and appreciation arise from allowing introspection, quietness and the recognition of emotions. During times of stillness it is safe to allow emotions to arise and allow inner-doubts and fears to be recognized and in the recognition, release and resolution begins. As the bond of love and trust grows, thoughts, fears and troubling emotions can be discussed with one another openly, new depths of love are attained and become expressions that are part of your daily life. Those who regularly experience times of silence in their lives experience less conflict. As you choose to release inner conflict, your outer world reflects this. You will find yourself feeling more peaceful and compassionate.

Taking time to allow yourself to tap into your emotions in stillness is beneficial. Taking time to communicate your emotions to your wife strengthens the bonds between you bringing understanding, comfort and true companionship which are the hallmarks of a satisfying relationship.

You and your fiancée may have been living together for a long time before the actual wedding. Even though this arrangement seems like married life, there is a subtle change that occurs once the vows have been exchanged. It is a beautiful change, a deepening of trust and commitment. As you move into your role as husband, you have the opportunity to explore, know and accept your inner being and the process of personal growth in the presence of another. You have the opportunity to express the deepest parts of yourself, confident of unconditional love and acceptance. By offering this same opportunity to your wife, you fulfill a vital role as a loving husband.

WORKSHEET FOR GROOMS PREPARATION

After reading the chapter, "For the Groom," take time to write any insights, thoughts, visions, and new awareness's you experienced as you practiced the various exercises suggested in the chapter. The expansions you experience in your consciousness will help you on your path of personal evolution and assist you as you become part of a loving, committed relationship.

The Night Before The Wedding;

An old tradition worth observing

The rehearsal dinner is over, the bride and groom say goodnight to the wedding party and to one another. They part reluctantly, each going to their own room and their own bed alone. The bride and groom spend this night before their wedding and the hours before the wedding the following day, apart.

There is much to be said about the tradition of the bride and groom staying apart the night before and the hours leading up to the wedding. They do not see one another until the bride appears at the end of the aisle. The groom waits in his finery at the altar and the bride, transformed into a vision of the Goddess, appears and slowly makes her way to stand beside her consort, on his left side next to his heart. This moment is infused with magic. The brief separation of a few hours, transforms everyday reality into an altered reality filled with grace, anticipation and sacredness.

This is a highly symbolic moment and marks the beginning of your transformation into a married couple. Each sees the other, as if for the very first time, recognizing both the outer beauty and the inner beauty as they look into one another's eyes and join hands and hearts.

I have attended weddings where the bride and groom are mingling with the guests before the wedding. It has been my experience that this degrades, to some degree, the magic of this momentous occasion. It's like a regular day, a regular party, when in fact it is the day holding within it a life enhancing ritual of transformation.

I urge brides and grooms to appoint their attendants to take care of guests, musicians and caterers the day of the wedding. Bride and groom remain apart from one another preparing physically and emotionally for the ceremony.

PART II

THE WEDDING CEREMONIES

Presenting: The Journey of Love

When a couple make vows to one another during the wedding ceremony, they are promising to join their lives together, not as two halves creating a whole, but as two whole beings creating a relationship of beauty and support. The magical and sacred journey through marriage is a path of loving acceptance. In the shelter of a marriage filled with loving trust, each partner can witness, acknowledge and support the processes of personal growth. It is within this relationship that individual potential is honored.

The wedding script, The Journey of love, gives voice to the awareness of bride and groom of their responsibility for their own inner joy, the respect due to one another and the trust needed along the path of the sacred journey. This script is extremely beautiful, powerful and moving. Those with great love and awareness begin their marriage with the journey of love.

The Journey of Love Wedding Ceremony

Convocation

Today, we are here as *Bride* and *Groom*, hand in hand stand at the gateway to the magical journey through time, the sacred journey into marriage. It is our loving wish that their journey be one of unending joy, personal growth and discovery. *Bride* and *Groom* are grateful that you are here, lending your love and support to them and look forward to your presence in their lives through the years to come.

To Bride and Groom

The process of creating your life together begins now. As you encounter the many changes that will occur as you travel through life together, be gentle with yourself, be gentle with one another. Let the process of becoming co-creators in life open your hearts to one another, to your families and your friends. Let yourself go on this journey of discovery trusting the vision you have for your life together. Let each day and each moment bring you closer to your connection to universal love.

Invocation

Today we call upon love. The energy of love is like a golden thread running through our lives. We cannot control this energy we can only open our hearts to it. As we invoke love we open to giving and receiving. We open our eyes and see universal love all around us. This powerful living force runs through us and leads us to our highest good. Today we welcome and honor the guidance of our hearts.

Consecration

Bride and *Groom* joyfully move into the sacred space of marriage. The vows they take here today will be written on their hearts. Beyond thought, beyond desire, the deep commitment that is marriage joins them together as one in spirit. Today they take the first steps on a journey of great joy, compassion and learning, giving and receiving. As bride and groom make their vows to one another today, let us all take a moment to renew vows of love, compassion, generosity and openness to those who travel with us on the journey of our lives. We can choose to view all our relationships as sacred through the power of love.

Vows: Bride and groom can make their personal vows here if they choose.

Statement of Intention

To groom: With a deep awareness of who you are and a deep appreciation for *bride*, do you take *Bride* to travel on this journey of life with you as a lifelong loving companion, an equal partner, lover, and wife.

I DO.

To bride: With a deep awareness of who you are and a deep appreciation for *Groom*, do you take *Groom* to travel on this journey of life with you as a lifelong loving companion, an equal partner, lover and husband.

I DO.

Exchange of rings

These rings are Circles of love connecting your hearts and lives together. They say that you are committed to one another in perfect love and trust through the sacred vows you have taken.

To Groom: Place the ring on *Brides* finger and repeat after me. I give you this ring as a symbol of my never ending love and my commitment to our lifelong journey together.

To Bride: Place the ring on *Grooms* finger and repeat after me. I give you this ring as a symbol of my never ending love and my commitment to our lifelong journey together.

Final Blessing

May you grow in peace and harmony throughout your life together as you continue in your commitment to loving yourselves and each other. May you empower one another through the years and enjoy the journey of love.

Proclamation of Marriage

As you, *bride* and you, *groom* have spoken vows of commitment and exchanged wedding ring, it is my great pleasure to pronounce that you are husband and wife.

You may KISS

Ladies and gentlemen Mr. and Mrs. _____

Presenting the Wedding of Joy and Bliss

This ceremony beautifully and poetically invokes the spirit of joy that is love. The words throughout the ceremony speak of openness, awareness, acceptance and joy, the elements of the true marriage. Stillness and the opening of the heart are components in this script. A sacred circle of love is created in this ceremony and all who enter this portal are filled with blessings.

The Wedding Of Joy And Bliss

Opening Words

We are here to celebrate a joyous occasion, the marriage of *Bride and Groom*. We delight in sharing their happiness as we recognize and enjoy the bliss of opening our hearts to love.

To The Bride and Groom

Today you stand together, in the presence of friends and family, committing to share your lives with one another. All of your friends and family with us today, join with me in wishing your days be filled with love, laughter, respect and compassion. May the joy you share today deepen and expand in an ever widening circle embracing your family and friends through the years.

To all of you here making this day a special celebration through your loving presence, bride and groom are grateful for your love and support.

Remembrance: (optional)

At this time, *Bride and Groom* would like to remember their loved ones who could not be with them today. *Bride* remembers her loved ones (*brides loved ones may be named*). *Groom* remembers his loved ones. *(Grooms loved ones may be named)* In remembering our loved ones, in living a life of love and fulfillment, we create a bridge through time, honoring our ancestors as we create a legacy for those who follow us.

Convocation and Blessing

May the blessings of your friends and family and your dedication to growing together through the years, strengthen your union with endurance, fidelity, honesty, understanding and kindness. You enter into this union with open hearts and your intention to fill your lives with true communication of heart, mind, body and soul. These intentions are magnified and blessed by all present today. May your hearts and souls evolve together through the sacred bond of marriage.

Today you commit to share your lives, yet remain true to your own individual selves, creating together a marriage of beauty and trust, joy and bliss. Within this hallowed space of love and acceptance, individuality is honored.

Invocation

Let us become quiet for a few moments as we become aware of the presence of the Spirit of Joy that is Love. This awareness fills our hearts and minds with abundant blessings. We invoke this joyful spiritual energy to infuse the lives of *Bride* and *Groom* and to uplift each of us as we allow kindness, understanding, gentleness and compassion to light our lives. May we live a heart centered life filled with love and the awareness of our oneness with all that is.

Today we honor the loving bond between *Bride and Groom*. Let us envision them forever infused with the radiant light of love, always enfolded in joy and ever blissful in each other's company. As they move through the years, may the infinite spectrum of eternal light bless them with the vision to behold one another most clearly, truly hear one another and nourish each other with tenderness.

May the vows you make here today be ever present, written within your hearts.

Vows

Personal vows may be exchanged here.

Statement of Intention (*optional if there are personal vows exchanged*)

Bride: Do you, *Bride*, take *Groom*, to be your husband, your cherished friend, your lover, and your companion as you grow in wisdom, sharing your love, joy and bliss throughout your life? Bride:

I do.

Groom: Do you, *Groom*, take *Bride* to be your wife, your cherished friend, your lover, and your companion as you grow in wisdom, sharing your love, joy and bliss throughout your life?

I do.

Blessing of the Rings

These rings, made of precious metals, formed in a circle, symbolize your joyful and never ending love. May they be a forever reminder of the loving words expressed here today and the sacred bond of your vows. Your wedding rings say that, even in your individuality, you belong to one another.

Exchange of Rings:

Repeat after Celebrant:

Groom to bride: I *Groom* give you this ring with great joy that you are my wife; it symbolizes my love and our sacred bond.

Bride to Groom: I *bride* give you this ring with great joy that you are my husband; it symbolizes my love and our sacred bond.

Pronouncement of Marriage:

As the two of you have promised your love and commitment to one another through the exchange of vows and the gift of rings, it is my privilege and great joy to pronounce you are husband and wife.

You may now kiss.

Ladies and Gentlemen, Mr. and Mrs. _____.

Presenting The Spirit Of Love Ceremony

This wedding ceremony speaks of the awareness that *Bride* and *Groom* are joining their physical lives and also joining together as two spiritual beings. The eternal nature of love and the beauty and joy in the inherent knowledge that we are all one is celebrated in this wedding ceremony.

The Spirit Of Love
Wedding Ceremony

Convocation:

Friends and Family we are here today to celebrate love. *Bride* and *Groom* are the reminders to all of us today that love is alive in the world.

Invocation:

The spirit of love is here within each of our hearts. Let us invoke the wisdom inherent in the realization of love. A sense of joy and wonderment accompanies this realization and also a sense of relief as the awareness that we are all one in love awakens in our hearts. Today is a day celebrating love!

May the golden threads of love running from heart to heart throughout the world, be strengthened on this day as we celebrate the love of *Bride* and *Groom*.

The Address:

A happy marriage consists of accepting that you are simultaneously united and separate. You choose today and every day of your life together to be united. Your lives are entwined; you share the love of your bodies, your thoughts, dreams fears and fantasies. However, each spirit grows at its own pace, in its own way. Allow space in your life together, so each may touch the indwelling spirit within and feel the connection to their guiding spirit. By taking time to be with yourself in quietness, in meditation, in communion with your own spirit, more awareness awakens and there is more love, insight and spiritual energy to share with one another. Welcome times of comfortable silence with one another, feeling the spirit of love move between you. Take time to be with friends, to share confidences with others, to laugh and enjoy community. Your continued connection to yourself as a spiritual being will enrich your relationship and your lives throughout the years.

Consecration:

Let us be still for a moment and open ourselves to the highest spirit of love, the divine energy of the universe. We place our trust in the guidance, goodness, healing and unconditional love available to each of us. Opening ourselves to this divine energy, we step into a higher octave of love. This higher octave allows us to love and accept ourselves and others unconditionally. We willing allow our hearts to be broken open that we may share in deeper and more gratifying ways the love that is our true state of being. As *bride and groom* stand within this sacred circle of love, we ask that the divine energy of universal love inform their lives together, filling them with blessings.

And so it is.

Statement of Intention:

The Vows: I, *Bride*, take you, *Groom* as my husband, seeing you as both man and as the radiant eternal spirit that dwells within you. I promise to love and honor you as my husband and always recognize and honor your eternal spirit.

I, *Groom*, take you, *Bride* as my wife, seeing you as both woman and as the radiant eternal spirit that dwells within you. I promise to love and honor you as my wife and always recognize and honor your eternal spirit.

The Blessing of the Rings

These rings are made of precious metals as brilliant as the stars. May their light shine as a reminder of your love and your eternal natures.

Groom to Bride: I give you this ring as a symbol of my never ending love for you, I ask that you wear it as my wife that all may know of my love for you.

Bride to Groom: I give you this ring as a symbol of my never ending love for you, I ask that you wear it as my husband that all may know of my love for you.

As you *Bride and Groom*, have declared your love for one another and your recognition of the eternal spirits that you are, vowing to love one another and exchanging rings as an outward symbol of your love it is my pleasure to pronounce that you are now husband and wife.

You may kiss.

Ladies and gentlemen Mr. and Mrs. _____

Presenting The Wedding Of Positive Vision

In creating the words of your marriage ceremony, it is important to use words of positive intention. It has been scientifically proven that your thoughts and words have the power to shape your reality. By focusing on positive thoughts and words, you are moved to positive, creative actions, which are the building blocks for your life.

Let your wedding vows state that even in times of stress and challenge, your thoughts will be of solutions, your words will be encouraging and, together, you will hold a vision of positive outcome. As you focus on the good, the beneficial, the complete, you create together a life of joy, prosperity, love and great reward

The Wedding Of Positive Vision

We are gathered here today to celebrate the joyous union of *Bride* and *Groom*. We all share in their joy and extend our love and best wishes to them.

To Couple

This ceremony brings you together as partners in life. On this day you joyfully and with great enthusiasm, commit to love one another unconditionally, allow one another the space to grow and flourish within your relationship and to honor your co-creative power. Today as you join your hands, hearts and spirits together, may you move forward into a life filled with understanding, compassion and great joy.

Remembrance

Bride and *Groom* wish to acknowledge the spirit of those loved ones who have departed. The love, wisdom and guidance they provided are greatly appreciated and their presence is sorely missed.

Invocation

Today we call upon Universal Spirit to guide and protect *Bride* and *Groom* as they move into their life together. *Bride* and *Groom*, call upon their higher selves to be present and assist in this sacred ritual of love and commitment. We invoke the awareness of love beyond the physical, love that recognizes and encompasses the eternal spirits of us all. It is through the acknowledgement of our higher eternal selves that we evolve into the transformational awareness that we are all one in love.

The Address

Bride and *Groom* are filled with hopes, dreams and plans for their future together. Remember as you go through life that your dreams are fulfilled to the degree that you allow life to move you gently downstream. The power of manifesting the life you truly want is available to you every day. The challenges which arise along the path of life are potentials for growth. In trusting your own powers of love and manifestation, you create together a life of great beauty filled with wisdom and patience. Remember to always speak about that which you do want, that which you love and admire in one another and in the world around you. Focus on the best, the highest outcome in every situation and plan only for the good. The formula of positive thoughts and words creates an emotional state that is receptive and attracts a positive fulfilling life. Allow your emotional balance, awareness and receptivity to carry you downstream where dreams are manifested through the power of your trust in your co-creative energy and your acceptance of the flow of universal love.

Expression of Intent

Bride and *Groom* have shared their life stories with one another. They have expressed their hopes and dreams. Today they are here with full hearts to recognize the bond between them and the vision they have of their life together. *Bride* and *Groom* ask that as they exchange vows, friends and family present today, reach into the chambers of their hearts to recommit their own vows of love to the relationships in their lives.

Personal Vows can be spoken here

To Bride: Do you bride now take groom to be your husband, your co-creative partner in life, your lover and your trusted friend.

I do.

To Groom: Do you groom now take bride to be your wife, your co-creative partner in life, your lover and your trusted friend?

I do.

Blessings of the Rings

These circles made of precious metals represent the strength of your bond, the great capacity the two of you have for creating a fulfilling life. Let these never ending circles be symbols in your life of the beauty of your love and your acceptance of one another. May the strength of the unbroken circle be the template for your life together.

Exchange of Rings

Groom to Bride: I give you this ring and ask that you wear it as a symbol of our bond of love.

Bride to Groom: I give you this ring and ask that you wear it as a symbol of our bond of love.

The Proclamation of Marriage

Bride and *Groom* you have trusted the guidance of your hearts and vowed to love one another tenderly and truthfully. As you have also given rings as a symbol of your love and commitment, it is my joyful duty to proclaim that you are now husband and wife.

You may now kiss.

Ladies and Gentlemen Mr. and Mrs. _____

Presenting The Handfasting Ceremony

The Celtic tradition of Handfasting began centuries ago when a couple who wished to be married, held hands in front of witnesses and pronounced their intention to live together as man and wife. This was often done when the brides' family was not wealthy enough to provide a dowry. With the spread of Christianity, this practice was abandoned as the church frowned on couples proclaiming themselves married without the benefit of clergy.

Today the ancient practice of handfasting is enjoying renewed interest. Handfasting is a beautiful symbolic ceremony using a cord, braided ribbons or scarf tied to the right wrists of the bride and groom, joining them together. Words of love and commitment are spoken. The handfasting ritual can be incorporated into a wedding ceremony and your bridal party and guests can participate.

Handfasting ceremonies stand on their own as a marriage ceremony if a legal representative signs the marriage license. Some couples choose the original meaning of the handfasting ceremony, which was committing to live together for a year and a day. At the end of the year and a day, they would decide to have a formal wedding or renew their handfasting vows for another year and a day. Today's couples sometimes choose to say they will live together as long as love shall last.

Handfasting is also an excellent way for gay or lesbian couples to make their commitment known, speak meaningful vows and have a ceremony celebrating their union.

The handfasting ritual can be performed as a Celtic ceremony incorporating the elements of the ancient world; earth, air, fire, water the spirit above and the spirit below (father sky and mother earth). This ceremony is performed in a circle.

The ritual begins with the element of air which is symbolized by the burning of sage, sweet grass or incense. The celebrant "smudges" the couple individually by gently waving the smoking sage around them. The sweet smelling smoke of the sage dispels any negative energy and fills the aura with strength and purity. The members of the wedding party, the family and those in the circle may also be smudged with sage.

The element of fire is called upon as the couple lights a candle together. While air symbolizes clear communication, fire symbolizes passion and transformation.

The next element to be invoked is water. The celebrant may anoint the couple with water from a sacred well or river, or water that has been infused with crystals and gemstones. The element of water symbolizes deep emotional commitment.

The last of the elements symbolically represented is earth, the symbol of stability. The element of earth can be symbolized by salt sprinkled at the couple's feet or the couple may plant a small tree or pot of herbs together.

Family and friends can be included in the invocation of each element through the sharing of a chalice of wine or water, the lighting of one candle from another around the circle, everyone participating in planting a pot of herbs. Handfasting ceremonies can be extremely creative and inclusive.

If the couple chooses, they can have different friends or relatives in the circle come up and wrap the cord once around their wrists.

This symbolizes the support of their whole community. The cords can be tied in a figure eight or the infinity symbol around the wrists and removed still tied together as a keepsake for the couple.

The Handfasting cord is traditionally four to six feet in length, often braided using two to six ribbons, silk ropes or beautiful fabric. Small charms can be braided into the cord symbolizing good fortune. The colors of the cord can be the combined astrological colors of the bride and groom or any of their favorite combinations.

Poetry, song and music are always welcomed at the handfasting ceremony. A fun way to end the ceremony; each person in the circle is given a small bell. As the bride and groom kiss at the end of the ritual, the bells are rung. This ends the ceremony on a note of magic.

Handfasting/Wedding Of
The Four Elements

Invocation

We are gathered here today to bless and celebrate the love between
_____ and _____. In celebrating their union, we summon the
sacred fabric of our world, the ancient elements, to symbolize and
strengthen the blessings bestowed upon their union.

(*The element of air is symbolized by smoke*) The celebrant takes the
burning sage or incense from the altar and wafts the smoke around
the couple.

To the East: We ask that this union be blessed with sincere
communication of the heart, genuine communication of mind and
tender communication of body. May each dawn be a fresh beginning
filled with joy. By the sharing of peaceful silence, may their union
be blessed with profound understanding. May the element of air
strengthen the bonds between _____ and _____.

(*The south is the element of fire*) Celebrant lights the candle on the
altar or the couple may light the candle together.

To the South: We ask that this union be blessed with warm embraces, the healing warmth of the hearth as it welcomes them home and the heat of love's passion. May the light created by both, illumine the seasons of shadows. May the element of fire strengthen the bond between _____ and _____.

(the west is the element of water) Celebrant anoints forehead of bride and groom with water from a sacred well or water that has been imbued with the energy of gemstones and crystals.

To the West: We ask that this union be blessed by the easy gentle flow of the rivers, the ancient wisdom of the creatures of the deep oceans, the serenity of the lake and the cleansing of the rains. May the element of water strengthen the bond between _____ and _____.

(The north is the element of Earth) Celebrant sprinkles salt at the feet of bride and groom.

To the North: We ask that this union be blessed with endurance and devotion. May Mother Earth fill _____ and _____ with the strength and purpose to grow within a lasting relationship, enriching your lives with fertility and blessing you with a home that is a haven of love, forgiveness and acceptance. May the element of earth strengthen the bonds between _____ and _____

Earth and Fire, Water and Air, all the elements remain true to their own nature yet together create a world of unity and beauty, today _____ and _____ commit to remain true to their own natures, yet create together a relationship of great beauty. May individuality reign within their oneness.

Bindings

_____ and _____ have chosen to be handfast today as an outward symbol of their marriage.

A cord, scarf or ribbons that you have braided together are used at this time for the handfasting. Your right hands are joined and the cord is layed over the wrists and tied after each question is answered.

The First Binding

Celebrant: Will you cause each other heartache?

Couples Response: We May.

Celebrant: Is that your intent?

Couples Response: No.

Celebrant: Will you be aware of one another's heartache and seek to ease it?

Couples Response: We will.

Celebrant: And so the binding is made

Celebrant: Lays the cord over the couple's wrists. A relative or friend may come forward to tie the cord.

The Second Binding

Celebrant: Will you share each other's joy?

Couple: We will

Celebrant: Will you hold a positive vision of life and of one another?

Couple: We will.

Celebrant: And so the second binding is made.

Celebrant lays the second cord over the joined hands. A relative or friend may come forward to tie the cord.

The Third Binding

Celebrant: Will you share your hopes and visions for your life together?

Couple: We will.

Celebrant: Will you work together, co-creating the manifestation of your life and dreams?

Couple: We will.

Celebrant: And so the third binding is made.

Celebrant lays the third cord over the joined hands. A relative or friend may come forward to tie the cord.

The Fourth Binding

Celebrant: Will you honor and hold sacred your binding to one another?

Couple: We will

Celebrant: And so the fourth binding is made

Celebrant lays the forth cord over the joined hands. A relative may come forward to tie the final knot.

Celebrant: With the fashioning of these knots all the positive desires, dreams, love, and happiness wished for you here today is bound to your lives. With the fashioning of these knots your vows of love, support for one another, and your willingness to share in the co-creative process of your life together is made real and true.

Unties the cord and removes it. If the figure eight configuration has been made, the cord is removed as one piece in the shape of the figure eight or infinity symbol.

The Couple may then exchange rings: *The exchange of rings is not a necessary component in the handfasting ceremony*

A RING BLESSING: These rings are made of precious metals, formed in a circle symbolizing the eternal nature of your love and the vows taken here today Each ring is a key to the others heart where love and acceptance always reside.

Groom to bride: I offer you this ring as a symbol of our sacred bond, so all may know of my love for you.

Bride to Groom: I offer you this ring as a symbol of our sacred bond, so all may know of my love for you.

PRONOUNCEMENT OF MARRIAGE: Because you have chosen one another and expressed your love and commitment through the binding of the handfasting cord and honored each other with the precious gift of rings, it gives me great pleasure to pronounce you are now husband and wife. You may kiss.

PRONOUNCEMENT OF HANDFASTING: if the couple is handfasting and not entering into a legal marriage, the statement would read, I now pronounce you handfast for a year and a day or I now pronounce you handfast for as long as love may last.

KISS

Ladies and Gentlemen Mr and Mrs. _____

The Grandmother's Wedding Prayer

We call upon the Spirit of Oneness some call God, some recognize as the essence of Love. This eternal energy is with us today bestowing goodness and mercy upon us and especially upon *bride and groom*.

Today, we call upon the Almighty Spirit of Love to fill all those who stand with the *bride and groom*. (Here the members of the wedding party may be mentioned) May this Spirit awaken a new depth of love and understanding in their lives. I thank you who stand with my (grandson/granddaughter) today for the friendship you have given to him/her, the support , acceptance and love you have shown him/her through the years.

As *bride and groom* offer their gift of love to each other, we recognize there is no greater gift than unconditional love, the great treasure which allows knowledge and acceptance of the very essence of one another.

We pray that their days be richly blessed with joy and peace, throughout their morning path, which begins today, through the noontime of their marriage, filling their lives with understanding and peace. As the night of their marriage approaches may they be filled with grace and wisdom, taking solace in the strength and longevity of their love.

We ask a blessing today on my (grandson/granddaughter) and his/her new spouse . May they have many years together and a happy and fruitful marriage.

PART III

THE UNITY RITUALS

Benefits Of The Unity Rituals

The Unity Ritual adds another dimension to the wedding ceremony. By including outward symbols of the inner process of marriage a greater imprint is made on the consciousness of the bride and groom.

The lighting of a candle, the combining of wines, sand or stones, the receiving of blessings through the ring warming ceremony and the symbolic jumping into their married life as they jump the broom are catalysts to strengthen the marriage bonds. The friends and family gathered to witness the wedding are often included in these unity ceremonies, creating a stronger foundation of support for the couple.

Most newly married couples want and need the presence, support and love of their families and friends. Both bride and groom want to feel that they are now part of a larger family. The Unity rituals begin or deepen the process of acceptance, patience, kindness and generosity towards the new family member extended family and friends. These connections makes for a fuller, more connected, more heart centered life. Bringing family members and friends into the ceremony through participation in the Unity Ritual or by having them read favorite passages or poems during the ceremony are ways to create a fuller more inclusive ritual and a deeper bond with your community of family and friends.

Let The Light Of Your Love Be A Beacon
Of Strength Shining
Through The Years.

Unity Candle Ritual

This ritual is perfect for an indoor wedding. Gusty winds or even a gentle breeze can be a detriment to lighting candles in outdoor ceremonies. Having large glass chimneys over the candles is one way to adapt the unity candle ceremony for outdoor use.

My favorite form of the Unity Candle Ceremony is one in which everyone participates.

1. Each guests receives a small candle as they are seated for the ceremony. When the time for the candle lighting ceremony, two friends or family members stand at the end of the last aisle of guests. Holding a lit taper, they light the candle of the guest seated on the aisle. Each guest passes the flame to the candle next to them. The flame makes its way through the guests to the parents of the bride and groom. They rise and light the two tapers on the Unity Candle table. The bride and groom take the two tapers and light the unity candle together. The guests can then extinguish their candles. The Unity candle burns throughout the rest of the ceremony filled with the love and good intentions of the guests and family members.

This form is very beautiful during a handfasting ceremony where the guests are standing or seated in a circle and the bride and groom are in the center.

2. In this form, the parents of the bride and groom participate

   A small table with a central pillar candle is set near the bride and groom. Two taper candles flank the pillar candle. A small votive candle is lit prior to the ceremony and is set on the table. The bride and groom turn towards the table. The mother and father of both the bride and groom stand and approach the table. Each father lights one taper. The mothers remove the tapers and hand one to the bride and groom. Each take a taper and light the central pillar candle.

Celebrant: "This candle ceremony represents the bride and grooms journey through their individual lives to the unity of their marriage. The taper candles represent the essence of who they were before they met, the lives they were born into and lived with their parents."

Bride and groom receive a taper from their mothers and light the central candle together symbolizing the joining of their separate lives.

"May the flame of love grow brighter in the hearts of bride and groom
and become a beacon of strength,
a light shining brightly through the years."

3. In this form, only the mothers participate. Another option for the Unity Candle Ritual is to invite the mothers to come to the candle table. The bride and groom each light a taper and hand them to their mothers. The mothers then light the central candle representing the joining of the two families.

Let us create a sacred foundation of beauty and love
on which to build our lives

The Sand Pouring Ritual

This is a fun ceremony in which all family members can be included. The grandparents, parents, beloved aunts and uncles, sisters, brothers and children can all have a part in the Sand Ceremony.

A decorative jar or vase with a cover is a perfect vessel for the sand.

The colors used in the wedding can be incorporated into the sand ritual.

Smaller jars of sand filled with a variety of colored sand surround the large jar. There should be one small jar for each person participating in the ceremony.

The grandparents or parents pour first, each pour sand into the bottom of the vessel. This symbolizes the foundation of the family.

Each family member then pours another layer of sand. If there are children from previous marriage, they pour just before the bride and groom.

Finishing the sand ritual, the bride and groom can pour their sand individually or together. This ritual results in a beautiful vessel with a rainbow of layered sand.

Another method is to have all family members pour the sand simultaneously into a large mouthed vessel. This method results in an interesting design with all the sand mingling, creating a multicolored artistic design.

The wedding celebrant will explain that each family member is pouring a symbol of their support and creating a foundation of family love and unity for the newlyweds to draw on.

These rings are filled with Blessings from
The warm hearts of your family
And friends

The Ring Warming Ritual

This is a beautiful ritual inviting the wedding guests, wedding party and the immediate family to bless and support the union of the bride and groom. It can include just the wedding party and parents of the bride and groom or may be extended to the guests depending on the number of guests and the time allowed.

After the wedding vows are exchanged, the celebrant requests the wedding rings. The celebrant holds the rings in her hand as she speaks a blessing. The rings are then handed to the maid of honor. She holds them in her hand and makes a verbal or silent blessing. She then passes them to the person next to her or to the mother of the bride who passes them to her husband or the person sitting next to her.

This is a wonderful time for a musical selection as the rings are being passed from guests to guest receiving blessings.

As the rings come to the mother of the groom, she stands and hands them to a groomsman or the best man. He adds his good intentions and hands them to the celebrant and the exchange of rings follows.

Each member of the family the bridal party and, if the bride and groom choose, each guests has an opportunity to imbue the wedding rings with good intentions for the new couple's life together.

These stones are symbols of your sacred connection to Mother Earth.
They carry the energy of unlimited possibilities and blessings

The Gemstone Ritual

The stones used in this ritual do not have to be expensive cut and polished stones but can be small raw or tumbled stones available at lapidary shops and craft stores. Each guest receives a small gemstone when they arrive at the wedding.

Stones such as quartz crystal, rose quartz, carnelian, jasper, amber, malachite, garnet, lapis lazuli and many others are perfect for the stone ritual as they carry a specific energy and their color adds vitality to the ceremony.

Each member of the wedding party carries a small gemstone with them during the processional. This stone holds a positive intention for the bride and groom. The stone is placed in a glass bowl on a table near the celebrant, a lit candle is also on the table along with a small drawstring bag made of velvet or lace. This bag can be in the colors matching the wedding theme.

The members of the bride and grooms families and the guests attending the wedding will be instructed by the celebrant to hold the stones and fill them with positive intentions and love for the bride and groom.

At a designated time during the ceremony, guests are invited to bring the stones to place in the bowl. While the stones are being placed in the bowl, a beautiful piece of music may be played. Some couples like to have everyone come up after the pronouncement of marriage where hugs and handshakes are exchanged. Others like this to be a more solemn moment taking place after the invocation.

After the exchange of rings, the bride and groom, together, place the stones in the velvet bag. The groom may hand them to the celebrant for a blessing such as "the gemstones within this bag, carry with them the energies of love, endurance, peace and prosperity. May they be a source of beauty and blessings in the lives of bride and groom and a source of beauty and inspiration in their home." The bag is then handed to the bride who easily carries them with her during the recessional.

Each gemstone has a specific energy and attribute. The energy of the stone will add strength to the intention held for the bride and groom.

- ♥ Red stones help to energize, balance and strengthen one's connection to the earth
- ♥ Clear stones or crystals bring clarity
- ♥ Moonstones gently stabilize emotional states and help relieve tension and stress.
- ♥ Yellow and orange stones assist with stability, creativity, clear thinking and the flow of life-energy through the body.
- ♥ Pink stones symbolize protection and unconditional love.
- ♥ Blue and green stones carry the energy of peacefulness.
- ♥ Turquoise stones assist with optimism and happiness.
- ♥ Purple and violet stones assist with change, growth and awareness.
- ♥ Multi-colored stones carry the energy of unlimited possibilities.

The stones can be placed in a decorative bowl in the couples' home, adorn a window sill where they can catch the light and fill the room with their energy. They can also be held in the hand during meditation. These stones, imbued with the love and positive intentions of friends and family, serve as a reminder of the community that loves and supports the couple.

New stones can be added through the years.

The Love Letter Ritual

This ritual actually begins a few weeks before the wedding ceremony.

The bride and groom separately compose love letters to one another. These letters express the love they are feeling as they approach their wedding day. The qualities that endear them to one another are included as well as the respect they hold for one another. The details of how they fell in love, their dedication to their future together, and their hopes and dreams are included in their letters to one another. These letters are sincere, personal and express the deepest emotions felt for one another. Each letter is put into a sealed envelope with the name of the beloved on the front. These letters are given to the mothers of the bride and groom to keep until the wedding day.

The next step in this ritual is to find, purchase or create a box for the love letters to be placed in during the wedding ceremony. The box should be something beautiful you can display in your home. It also has two locks on it.

At the rehearsal dinner or the night before the wedding, the couple can place in the box a nice bottle of wine, a piece of their favorite music, a photo of them as they were dating and falling in love. The love letter box, is a love time capsule.

During the wedding ceremony at a designated time, usually directly after the wedding vows, the two mothers walk up and place the love letters in the box. At this time the box is locked.

For the next five years, the beautiful love letter box maintains a place of honor in the home of the newlyweds. On their fifth anniversary, the couple unlock the box, read the letters they wrote to each other, share the bottle of wine and listen to their favorite song.

If before the fifth wedding anniversary the couple should hit a hard time in their relationship, before they give up on their marriage, they will open the love letter box. Each of them will go into a separate room and read the letter written to them before their wedding day. This love missive will remind them of all they mean to each other, the things they love about one another and the reason they married.

The love letter box is a beautiful ritual to include in your marriage ceremony, a wonderful way to spend your fifth wedding anniversary and a bit of love insurance if you should hit a rocky spot along your way.

The Planting Ritual

This is a beautiful and unique ceremony for an outdoor wedding and for those couples who want to include family members in the ceremony.

A decorative shallow planter with some soil in it is placed on a table near the celebrant. Surrounding the planter are small plants which have been removed from their containers and placed on paper napkins surrounding the planter. A small trowel is placed next to each plant. Plants can be chosen for the traits they symbolize such as;

- ♥ Sage for wisdom,
- ♥ Rosemary for remembrance,
- ♥ Thyme for steadfastness and
- ♥ Fern for undying love.

The bride and groom, their parents or any other friends or family they wish to include, gather around the table after the celebrants address or invocation. This is in the middle of the ceremony.

Each person places a plant in the planter, takes the trowel and puts the soil around it. As each person places a plant, they can choose to make a statement of support for the couple. The celebrant may state the attributes of each plant and explain briefly that the family is creating a unity planter which the bride and groom will nurture in their home.

May a bond of sweetness and strength
Be formed to sustain you through your years together
as husband and wife.

The Wine Ritual

To incorporate the wine ritual within your wedding ceremony you must have a small table set up near the celebrant where the ceremony will take place.

You may ask your maid of honor to carry a carafe of white wine during the processional and place it on the table.

The best man can carry the carafe of red wine and place it on the table. Another member of the wedding party can bring up the empty wine glass and place it on the table. If there is no wedding party, the table can be set up before the wedding with the carafe of red wine, the carafe of white wine and the empty wine glass.

After the wedding vows are spoken and the rings are exchanged, bride and groom stand next to the wine table. The groom pours a little red wine into the wine glass. The bride pours a little white wine into the glass. The wedding celebrant says "As these two wines combine, forming a new creation, a new and unique taste, so do bride and groom now join forming a bond of sweetness and strength to sustain them through their years together as man and wife."

The groom lifts the wine glass. He may make a toast to his new bride and then have a sip of the wine. He then hands the glass to the bride. She may make a toast to her new husband and take a sip of the wine. It is not necessary to make a toast at this time, but some couples feel moved to do so.

The couple returns to the celebrant where they receive the final blessing on their union, the celebrant announces they are husband and wife, they kiss and are introduced for the first time as husband and wife.

Jumping The Broom

Couples from all nationalities, belief systems and walks of life have incorporated this final ritual into their wedding.

A broom, its handle decorated with ribbons and charms, is laid on the ground in the aisle behind the bride and groom, in front of the first row of chairs. The broom symbolizes crossing the threshold into their new life together as a married couple. The charms decorating the broom are blessings for love, fertility, prosperity and long life.

After the proclamation of marriage, the bride and groom turn to face their friends and family. As they begin the recessional, they jump over the broom as they walk down the aisle into their new life together. The maid of honor or the best man picks up the broom and follows the bride and groom. The broom is kept by the bride and groom and can be displayed as an interesting piece of folk art in their home.

PART IV

YOUR' MARRIAGE IN THE STARS

The Wedding Chart

Ancient astrology was the first method developed to describe character. For centuries, couples preparing for marriage had their astrological charts read. This reading gave them an opportunity for a deeper look into their combined personalities, character traits, strengths and weaknesses. The chart also advised them as to which cosmic forces would be affecting the different areas of their life through the years. In some instances, the marriage was cancelled if the charts were not favorable for a happy and prosperous marriage.

While the use of Astrology is not a tool to dictate your lives, it provides an awareness which assists you in avoiding obstacles as your life unfolds. It confirms your connection and helps chart the course of your lives into a deeper and more thorough understanding of yourself and your relationship

Astrology is an ancient science and a fun way to gain insight and self-awareness. Knowing a bit about the sun sign, rising sign, moon sign and planetary configurations at the time of birth gives you a glimpse of the cosmology of your-self and your partner.

A good Astrologer can create a chart which combines the energy of both bride and groom's birth charts at the time of the wedding. This combined chart, called a synergy chart, serves as an overview of the greater forces at play in your lives. It reflects the personality, complexity and challenges of your partnership. The astrologer will interpret the meanings, changes and opportunities the synergy chart expresses.

The energies the planets stand for in the wedding chart are the same as in an individual reading, but they are considered from the point of view of how they affect the relationship. The following list is a very brief summary of the individual planetary energies.

- The *Sun* describes an individual's identity and purpose. In a relationship the Sun is the source of vitality.
- The *Moon* is representative of the emotions and how they are expressed, and in a relationship identifies the emotional response that one partner might make to the other.
- *Mercury* is the symbol of the mind, describing the individual's thought and communication patterns, and in a relationship shows the extent to which the partners are "on the same wavelength" and can communicate with each other.
- *Venus* is the Goddess of Love, and the energies of this planet represents the compatibility and friendliness of basic interactions, as well as the emotional component of sexual attraction.
- *Mars* symbolizes the will and vitality of an individual, and represents the balance of power that exists in any relationship, and potential threats to that balance, plus the physical aspects of sexual attraction.
- *Jupiter* is the traditional planet of individual expansion, in a relationship showing how partners can help each other grow and have new experiences.
- *Saturn* stands for duty and control, but also for stability.
- *Uranus* is the element of unpredictability and surprise that is necessary to keep any relationship alive, though its energies can also be disruptive.
- *Neptune* can symbolize both spiritual ideals and escapism, which can be opposite sides of the same urge to transcend.
- *Pluto* is the transformative factor, in which change often happens.

The astrological chart is presented in the form of a circle divided into twelve sections like a pie. Each section represents a house. A major part of a chart reading is the houses the planets fall in. There are twelve houses, and each house is associated with a particular necessity of life.

- The first house is associated with identity and self-expression. (Fire, Cardinal)
- The second house stands for wealth—both outer wealth and the inner wealth that comes from stable values—and with the need for security. (Earth, Fixed)
- The third house concerns the flow and communication of ideas—through learning, teaching, conversation and writing. (Air, Mutable)
- The fourth house is associated with "home," both the physical home that we live in, and the foundation established in our childhood home.. (Water, Cardinal)
- The fifth house is concerned with children, and with creativity, talent, play, and romance—the expression of which requires a child-like spontaneity. (Fire, Fixed)
- The sixth house is how we spend our day, our health, our daily tasks, work requirements and the attention that we bring to the routines that maintain this area of life. (Earth, Mutable)
- The seventh house is concerned with partnerships of all kinds, and one-to-one relationships (including that with a spouse), and our ability to manage those requirements. (Air, Cardinal)
- The eighth house is in general associated with what we share with others, and this can include the desire for meaningful relationship, sexual activity, money and possessions, even inheritances. (Water, Fixed)

- The ninth house includes foreign travel, religion, higher education, and other activities that broaden our horizons or enable us to develop a coherent individual philosophy of life. (Fire, Mutable)
- The tenth house stands for career, ambition, reputation and anything we do or want to do that gives us recognition or a public face. (Earth, Cardinal)
- The eleventh house includes social life, the need for friendship, shared interests, group activities, social causes, and how we are able to blend in with the needs of a group. (Air, Fixed)
- The twelfth house incorporates the need for self-discovery, self-acceptance, and individuation of the unconscious—as well as some of the pitfalls that can ensue (such as addiction, institutionalization) if this need is not met. (Water, Mutable)

I suggest that those interested in the information and insights a combined astrological chart will provide, contact a local astrologer of good reputation and make an appointment. You will need the date, time and place of your birth.

The Magic rose unfolds in a prism of mystic color
The beauty that it holds is the harmony between lovers.

Your Astrological Sun Sign, Flowers, Metals, Gemstones & Colors

Each sun sign has a special color, flower, gem stone and metal reflecting the planetary energy associated with the astrological sign. Wedding ceremonies by their very nature are symbolic. Incorporating the colors and flowers that are associated with the sun signs of the bride and groom are a fun way to bring a subtle but cosmic symbolism into the ceremony. Symbolism can be incorporated into almost every part of the ceremony, strengthening the emotional and energetic imprint. The flowers, candles, bridal bouquet, handfasting cord, sand used in the sand ritual, bridesmaid's dresses and groomsmen's ties can reflect the colors associated with the bride and groom astrological signs.

Aries—March 21 to April 20

Those born in the fiery sign of Aries are known for their enterprising spirits. No surprise that flowers representing them are tenacious, like the honeysuckle vine and thistles, hot and fast growing like peppermint and brightly colored like Tiger lilies.

- color most often associated with Aries is red
- Metals are gold and bronze
- Gemstones are Ruby, Red Jasper, Carnelian, Red Coral and Diamond.

Taurus—April 21 to May 20

Venus smiles on those born in the sign of the bull. Taurians traditionally love beauty and are well known for their determination.

Roses, considered the most beautiful flowers are symbols of Venus and thus known as the flower of both Taurus and Libra. Poppies and Foxgloves with their extravagant blooms speak of the Taurus energy of bounty and beauty.

- Colors most often associated with Taurus are deep yellow and sandy beige
- Metals are Silver, Gold and Copper
- Gemstones are Emerald, Golden Topaz and Agate

Gemini—May 21 to June 20

Those born under the sign of the twins are talkative, inquisitive and cheerful. They are known for their easy breezy attitudes and love of bright colors.

While brightly colored Chrysanthemums, yellow orchids and Azaleas stimulate the Gemini eye, Lavender is often needed to calm their exuberant spirit. Maiden hair ferns also offer beauty and a cooling effect.

- Colors most often associated with Gemini are yellow, violet and silver.
- Metals are Gold and Silver
- Gemstones are Crystal, Aquamarine, Alexandrite, Beryl and Pearl

Cancer—June 21 to July 20

Those born under the sign of Cancer are sensitive, perceptive, highly intuitive, sweet and endearing. When life gets uncomfortable, they can sometimes be a little crabby. They react to the pull of the moon and their emotions ebb and flow. The Cancerian loves family life and needs friends who can keep them grounded as their intuitive nature makes them a bit dreamy.

The white rose is associated with the sign of Cancer as is the Water Lily, Lotus, Southern Magnolias and Verbena.

- Color most often associated with Cancer is Sea Green.
- Metal is Silver
- Gemstones are Ruby, Moonstone, Pearl, Green turquoise.

Leo—July 21 to August 20

Leo lives life large. They love the spotlight, are theatrical and brilliant.

The sunflower is the ultimate Leo flower along with marigolds, Passion flowers, Dahlias and the aromatic Heliotrope. Bay, Laurel and Palm trees are all ruled by the sign of Leo.

- Color most often associated with Leo is Gold.
- Metal is Gold
- Gemstones are Amber, Sardonyx, Ruby, Jacinth and Peridot.

Virgo—August 21 to Sept. 20

Those born under the sign of the virgin are wonderful with details. They strive for perfection and are deeply caring.

Virgo rules Chrysanthemum, Narcissus and all brightly colored small flowers.

- Colors most often associated with Virgo are Purple, Deep Royal Blue.
- Metal is Gold.
- Gemstones are Pink Jasper, Rhodochrosite, Azurite, Sapphire, and Star Sapphire.

Libra—Sept. 21 to Oct. 20

"Beauty and balance, justice for all" is the mantra of those born under the sign of Libra. They want everyone to get along. Libra's enjoy a beautiful environment and take care to present themselves in the most beautiful light.

Large roses speak of the Libra energy as well as Daisies, Mint and Hydrangeas, all beautiful flowers to add to the bridal bouquet.

- Colors most often associated with Libra are light yellow and pink.
- All metals are ruled by Libra.
- Gemstones are Opal, Fire Agate, Agate and Tourmaline.

Scorpio—Oct. 21 to Nov. 20

Sign of mystery and intrigue, the highly intuitive Scorpio can be deeply spiritual and extremely intelligent.

Gardenias with their heady scent, heather and honeysuckle are ruled by Scorpio along with deep red flowers.

- Color most often associated with Scorpio is Crimson.
- Metals are Gold and Silver
- Gemstones are Topaz, Garnet, Coral, Ruby, Zircon

Sagittarius—Nov. 21 to Dec. 20

Never boring, these lovable archers love to travel, are deeply philosophical and outspoken.

Pink carnations and Peonies can represent Sagittarius in your flower arrangements. Also blackberries, mosses, sage and limes.

- Color most often associated with Sagittarius is Blue-Green
- Metals are Silver, Gold and Copper.
- Gemstones are Amethyst, Malachite, Zircon and Turquoise.

Capricorn—Dec.21 to Jan. 20

Those born under the sign of Capricorn are known for their longevity and ability to manifest wealth. Wisdom comes with age and they are the sages of the zodiac.

The Capricorn energy is represented by Ivy, Hemp, Camellias, Pansies, Heartsease and Magnolias. The earthy Capricorn can also be represented by branches, flowers or cones from Pines, Willow branches and Aspen leaves.

- Colors most often associated with Capricorn are Black and White
- Metals are Gold and Silver.
- Gemstones are Onyx, Quartz, Beryl, Jet, Garnet and Obsidian.

Aquarius—Jan. 21 to Feb. 20

Attuned to the greater good of all, Aquarians are inventive and expressive. The Aquarian mind is sharp and agile. They are of great benefit to their communities as they have the ability to see the big picture with compassion.

Orchids are beautiful in the Aquarian bride's bouquet as are Bird of Paradise for a dramatic effect. Trillium and Gladiolus are perfect in a trailing bouquet.

- Color most often associated with Aquarius is Electric Blue
- All metals are ruled by Aquarius
- Gemstones are Blue Sapphire, Lapis, Aquamarine and Amethyst

Pisces—Feb. 21 to March 20

Spiritual, intuitive, empathic and giving, the Pisces' qualities endear them to everyone.

Water lilies are their flower along with Moss, Lilac, Wisteria blooms, Willow branches and figs.

- Colors most often associated with Pisces are Soft Azure and Light Blue
- Metal is Silver
- Gemstones are Diamond, Turquoise, Jade, Tourmaline and Bloodstone

Be creative; express your most cosmic self through your flower choices and colors. Craft a ceremony filled with symbols of your spirituality, personalities and love and appreciation for one another.

PART V

THE JOURNEY TO SELF KEYS TO A JOYFUL MARRIAGE

Developing Heart Centered Awareness,

Building the rainbow bridge

Planning a wedding is a joyous occasion but, as we have discussed in this book previously, it can also have stressful components. Dealing with the various vendors can be challenging but even, more so, the emotions that arise as you go through the wedding planning can create a strain on your relationship and your relationship to parents, relatives and friends that are involved. It is with this scenario in mind, that I offer you the following tools.

In the previous chapters we have discussed the connection our thoughts have to our emotions and the benefits of meditation, becoming still and letting our minds rest as we breathe and make room for new awareness's. These are vital components in heart centered living.

Within this chapter the development and use of heart centered living is explained and explored. The stress of the wedding and the challenges and stressors of life can be managed with much more ease and also provide personal growth and a deeper bond between you, your fiancé, friends and family as heart centered living becomes a way of life.

Your emotions are the contact point between your physical being and your connection to the pure positive energy of all that is. This connection provides a powerful guidance system. Beyond your sense of taste, smell, hearing, vision and physical touch, there is a sixth sense, your emotions. By taking time to become aware of your feelings you make contact with this inner knowing. Your thoughts create the emotional feelings running through your body. When you allow your feelings to arise, notice that the thoughts you think change the way you feel. Making this contact is the first step in aligning with the guidance system of your heart, which is your connection to spiritual energy, God, your Higher Self, or the Power of Love.

I am not suggesting that if you have a fearful or angry thought you can magically whisk it away with good thoughts. For instance, you may feel comfortable with an angry feeling. This emotion may serve as a tool to assist you in setting boundaries. However, staying in anger blocks the flow of good into your life. When anger begins to drain your energy you will, naturally, want to move upward. You can begin to diffuse negative energy by becoming aware of the thoughts you are thinking and the feelings your thoughts evoke. Begin to allow and explore thoughts which bring emotional relief. As you follow the soothing thoughts, you are tapping into your guidance system. This awareness gently lifts you into a state of mind that is more in alignment with the way you want to feel.

As you become aware of your intention to feel better, the energy begins to move in the direction of your focus. By consciously allowing your feelings and exploring thoughts that soothe and thoughts that irritate you can chose to move up through your emotions arriving at a place of peace.

Your thoughts can move you

- ♥ from anxiety to anger,
- ♥ from anger to frustration,
- ♥ from frustration to boredom,
- ♥ from boredom to hope,
- ♥ from hope to creativeness,
- ♥ from creativeness to enjoyment,
- ♥ from enjoyment to happiness

It won't happen all at once. Moving yourself upwards may take time, as you must move at your own pace. For some the transition from one emotion to the next can happen in minutes, others may take hours or days to move up to a better emotional state. There is no limitation on the process and no judgment passed on this personal inner-work.

Benefits of Building the Rainbow Bridge from your thoughts to your emotions, to your connection with All That Is.

- ♥ Exploring your thoughts and progressing through your emotions, creates a center of confidence within you.
- ♥ You are no longer the victim of your emotions but can now use them as the powerful guidance system they are meant to be.
- ♥ Harnessing the power of positive thought and emotions lifts you into a place of confidence in your decisions and your intuition.
- ♥ Your emotional guidance system is your greatest ally. Developing awareness and listening to your emotions strengthens your personal power to create the marriage and the life you desire.
- ♥ Remember to breathe and allow the breath to calm the body as your thoughts have the ability to calm the emotions.

Consciously inviting and utilizing this guidance system in the marriage ceremony and into your life together brings more clarity and a deeper more resonant feeling of connection with yourself and one another. As feelings are acknowledged, misunderstandings are resolved and trust grows stronger. By feeling free to discuss the thoughts and beliefs that led to discord with your partner, without judgment, you can create together better feeling thoughts and a life of conscious connection.

This conscious emotional awareness is a practice that grows easier with time and may seem to become second nature during your ordinary daily life. However, during times of extreme stress you may need to remind yourself to employ this powerful tool. Practicing emotional awareness is a key component to happiness.

Focusing your intention on the life experience you want to create with your mate shifts you attention away from any negativity that may be occurring. This shift supports you own power and brings you into a more positive focus. The insights gained as you begin to see (or remember) your own power of creation enhances your life. With this knowledge, you hear with new ears the words you speak and the creative impact they have on you and your relationship. This awareness enhances your life as you realize you never have to be a victim of circumstances, as you are the creator of your own reality. Create your wedding day with joy, wonder, gratitude and love knowing that what you send out through your thoughts, words and actions is mirrored back to you and creates the joyful journey of your marriage.

When bride and groom have the capacity to call upon the inherent wisdom of the heart, they live from a place of awareness. They become two whole beings joined together to co-create a joyous, rewarding life filled with love and trust. I call this practice building the rainbow bridge. This bridge leads from anger, despair and irritation into gratitude, acceptance and the conscious creation of a heart centered life.

The Emotional Response Guide

This guide begins at the bottom with depression and moves up through the emotions that lead to joy and empowerment. Of course, we do not always begin at the bottom. Often, when we are not feeling happy, we are anxious or frustrated. This list is a tool to assist you in recognizing your emotional state and moving to the next, most comfortable, space you can achieve through your thoughts. Movement up the scale occurs when you relax, breathe and allow a thought to lead you, noticing when you begin to feel a sense of soothing. Lifting yourself into a soothed state you can experience compassion for yourself, release anxiety and enjoy the planning of your wedding. Learning to bring yourself into harmony and balance by following the guidance of your emotions is a tool that will serve you throughout your life.

- Joy/Empowerment
- Excitement
- Happiness
- Enthusiasm
- Co-operation
- Calmness/Acceptance
- Hope
- Boredom
- Frustration/irritation
- Apathy/overwhelm
- Disappointment
- Anger
- Blame
- Guilt
- Depression/Grief

Emotional Response Dialogues—
Putting it into Practice

When we become upset over an issue in our lives, our concerns can take over our minds and our emotions. This inner dialogue and the resulting emotional reactions create discord in our relationships and dis-ease in our bodies. Creating drama is very addictive; however, it does nothing for our relationships, our inner peace or our personal growth. Moving our awareness away from the cycle of negative thoughts and emotional reactions is the beginning of self-awareness and heart-centered living.

Becoming mindful of what you are thinking and deciding to move away from the negative inner dialogue into a more comfortable thought is the pathway to peace of mind and positive resolution of painful emotions. Sometimes not giving a lot of energy to a situation and focusing on something more positive is a resolution in itself. Being aware of our ego's need to always be right, always be the center of attention and always be acknowledged is beneficial. As we mature in our relationships with others and ourselves, recognizing and dismissing our ego's unreasonable demands, we become less reactive and better able to respond from our hearts.

Below are samples of inner dialogues. I have chosen to use simple examples of emotional states that may arise around the preparation for a wedding and a few months after the wedding.

It is very possible to go up the emotional scale and then fall back to a lower level, then move up once again. The important thing is your awareness and willingness to move into a better feeling. The internal dialogue below could take place within a ten minute span or a ten hour span. The speed with which you move depends on the situation you are dealing with and your ability and willingness to release what does not serve your highest good and move toward tranquility.

The Bride

The day of the rehearsal dinner the caterer calls and says the main dish you have chosen for the dinner is not available. You go into an emotional spin. Doubts plague your mind.

"I really wanted this dinner to be perfect. Now it is ruined." Grief

"I've chosen the wrong caterer, the dinner will be inedible." Anxiety

"I can't believe this guy! What incompetence! I will spread the word to everyone to never hire this company." Anger/hostility

"Of all the caterers in this city, I have to choose the most inept. I don't know what to do." Self blame/apathy

Growing more and more anxious, you decide to breathe and begin to bring yourself into alignment with a better feeling scenario.

"The most important thing about the dinner is that we are all together celebrating our love." Calmness/acceptance

"I can get the caterer to offer more hor's dourves before the dinner and select a better wine." Co-operation

"The replacement dish may be even better than the original one we chose." Acceptance

"My best friend from college whom I haven't seen in three years will be there and my cousins who I almost never see will be there too." Excitement

"This is the night before my wedding day. I will be seeing my fiancé for the last time before I walk down the aisle to become his wife. The dinner will be beautiful." Joy and empowerment.

The Groom

A few weeks before the wedding, you are feeling neglected. You are upset that your girlfriend is so involved in wedding plans that she totally ignores you. You are wondering if it is worth it. Have you made the right choice or are you making a big mistake?

"I can't believe she is totally ignoring me." Anger/insecurity

"I wonder if she even remembers who she is marrying." Anxiety

"How can she be angry with me because I don't want to talk about flower arrangements, I don't know anything about flower arraignments?" Frustration

"She is shouldering the responsibility for all the wedding decisions. I shouldn't be feeling like this." Guilt

"I miss spending time with her." Grief/loneliness

"If every time an event comes up in our life, I'm going to be tossed aside, I will be miserable." Frustration/futurizing

"We both need to understand that men and women do not always think the same way." Hopeful

"This will all be over in a few weeks. I can go hang out with my buddies and have a drink or two until then." Boredom

"Actually, while she is busy planning the wedding, I have time to finish up projects at work before the wedding date." Acceptance/Creativity

"I miss her, I can be more involved in the planning, she would like that." Cooperative

"An event this important does not come often in life." Calmness/Acceptance

"I want to see her happy and enjoying planning our wedding".
Empowerment

"I'm so in love with her and so glad to be getting married."
Excitement

"I'll call her and ask what I can do to help today." Co-operation

Six months later

You have been married for six months. You begin to feel that your new husband, Jake, is taking you for granted. His comments of loving appreciation of you, your beauty and talents are dwindling. The weekend he has to spend at the office finalizing a big project, you sit at home alone.

Inner dialogue:

"Married life is not what I expected. I had more fun when I was single. I feel like I'm becoming invisible to Jake." Boredom/ Grief

"I could go to the gourmet market and gets some things to make a really nice dinner tonight, but why bother? Jake will just come in and say he ate while he was working or not even notice the great meal I fix for him. He is so self-centered!" Frustration.

"I'm not going to worry about Jake today. I'm going to take a day just for me, starting with that yoga class I've been meaning to get to. Maybe that will get me out of this funk." Hope.

Arriving home from your yoga class you sink into a warm bath and enjoy the glow of the scented candles surrounding the bathtub.

"This feels great. I want to go to the yoga class more often and spend more time just relaxing and enjoying myself. It feels good to get back in touch with me again." Calmness/Acceptance

"Maybe my expectations of Jake are unreasonable. We both work hard, he is just as overwhelmed as I am. We need to take some time to discuss our feelings." Co-operation/Creativeness

"I had such a great time in my yoga class today, I am going to encourage Jake to get back to his weekly basketball game with his buddies. He hasn't seen them in months." Calmness/creativeness/happiness.

As you can see by reading through these short examples, thoughts can bring you into a state of anger, fear and frustration but they can also lift you into a new awareness and a state of allowing. This state of allowing is beneficial to you as it soothes you and opens your heart to greater understanding of yourself and others. Allowing is beneficial to your loved one as it grants him/her to experience freedom within your loving relationship and opens their heart in gratitude and deeper love. Staying in anger is detrimental to your health, your peace of mind and your relationships with everyone. Breathe deeply; allow compassion for yourself and others to guide you. Express kindness and encouragement to your mate. Sharing positive, loving acceptance creates a cycle of serenity and tranquility within your marriage.

The Journey To Self—
Keys To A Joyful Marriage

Most of you who are reading this book have found your partner and are preparing to marry. The information contained in this chapter is to assist you through your life together.

All of us want a lasting, loving, fulfilling relationship. As you enter into marriage your hearts are open and you know that all good things are possible. As you go through the weeks, months and years of your married life you come to understand that a lasting relationship and a happy and fulfilling marriage, begins with self-love and self-acceptance, the journey into your own inner being.

This journey begins when you consciously start to look within, acknowledge and accept your feelings and use them as a guiding voice in your life. Through the practice of meditation, or times of silence you gain insight into your feelings and the motivations they engender. This clarity helps to dissolve old imprints and makes room for new healthy awareness. Being attentive to your true feelings and accepting yourself with all of your flaws and fabulousness allows others to appreciate and embrace you as the open and authentic being you are. Gaining self-knowledge, self—love and self-acceptance brings you to a state of serenity. The more you know yourself the more personal power you feel. The outer world and whatever challenges arise are met with poise. It is in this state of poise, balanced between serenity and power, that your life is filled with conscious intention, compassion and wholeness, living in harmony with yourself, your beloved and the world.

Sharing your life with another who is willing to walk the path leading to self-awareness and self-love brings your life's journey into a higher octave. When two who are self-aware come together forming a bond in marriage, they complement and assist one another, allowing the process of self-exploration and integration to be part of their marriage. You share equal respect, love, honor and support. You no longer expect another to complete you but delight in the company of your divine complement. This relationship allows a heart to heart connection which grows stronger through the years, creating a matrix of love and wholeness that can be shared with family, friends and community.

The Journey to Self

1. Once again, I stress the importance of meditation. Meditation is facilitated by spending time in silence, by allowing your consciousness to go within. Lie down with your spine straight, breathe deeply and relax, close your eyes. When thoughts arise, bring the attention to the natural inhale and exhale of your breath. When the mind is quiet, you can open to the guidance of your inner being. Allow awareness to arise in silence and breathe into the places in your body or mind where fear blocks your journey within. When you first begin, you may only spend a few minutes in this deeply relaxed state, allowing yourself to become accustomed to the stillness. You may eventually choose a topic such as patience, kindness or gratitude to contemplate or you may develop the stillness within. As you continue to practice and become more comfortable with the process of letting go of extraneous thoughts you will

enjoy this time immensely. It is like taking time to clear the blackboard of old information and chalky dust. Once the board is clean, clarity, vital information and awareness can be appreciated and integrated.

2. Another simple exercise for inner work is to sit before a candle and stare into the flame. As distracting thoughts arise, acknowledge the thought and let it pass. You can watch it float away. Don't develop the thought or follow it, just let it go. Spending time in stillness allows the inner you to arise. You will be in touch with "the one" who knows you completely, the true feelings of your own inner being.

3. Traveling within is a powerful step. You may benefit greatly from the use of guided meditations to assist you in achieving deep relaxation and insights for personal growth. Guided meditations help to silence the inner chatter as your mind is focused on receiving suggestions for deep relaxation, inner peace, prosperity, and an allowing of all good things into your life.

4. Body awareness is another important ingredient. Yoga is a wonderful tool for body awareness. The slow stretches and balanced poses bring your awareness to wear you are holding tension in your body. Knowing where your energy is blocked is the first step in releasing the energy. Achieving balance within the body assists with balance within the mind. You may choose to explore Qi Gong, Tai Chi and dance as avenues to body awareness.

5. Sharing your concerns with another is also a way to self—knowledge and personal growth. You may have

a grandmother, therapist or friend you feel comfortable with. You know who you can really talk to. Getting feedback and insights from a trusted confidant is helpful in moving into a self-aware consciousness.

When asking for feedback and advice, put aside your ego, that part of you that cannot hear negative things about yourself. This is an important part in achieving freedom and recognizing the ways you self-sabotage and alienate others. Being willing to consciously open your awareness and make changes that are beneficial to you is a key ingredient in self-growth. You may feel angry or hurt when the one you trusted to share your inner self with points out behaviors that seem to be an ingrained part of who you are, but, nonetheless, do not serve your highest good and greatest potential. When you willingly allow yourself to witness your reaction, realizing that this is your ego, which always must be right, rearing its destructive head, you can laugh at the attempt at self-sabotage and move into a higher state of self-awareness. Knowing who you are and knowing who you wish to become, allows you to release old ego driven patterns and brings you to a state of personal awareness, acceptance and love. This is the one who can be a true partner in life and appreciate the beauty of another who is self-aware, self-accepting and willing to continue to work towards wholeness with you.

6. Self-talk. As you become aware of your inner dialogue through meditation and contemplation you have the opportunity to change your self-talk. You can train your thoughts to reflect your desires and envision, through words and thoughts, positive outcomes as you move through your life's journey. Speaking of what you do

want, seeing solutions, and maintaining a positive and happy attitude is the recipe for attracting a fulfilling life. As you and your partner share positive conversation, hold positive vision and take positive actions you create a life of great joy and fulfillment. Training the inner dialogue to reflect the most positive outcome for yourself is an exercise that will change your life.

Listening to your inner self has enormous impact on your life and the fulfillment you can achieve. Being comfortable with who you are, allows others to be comfortable with you. Knowing who you are brings a sense of self—respect and assists you in setting healthy boundaries.

Contemplation, guided meditation, body awareness, counseling and becoming aware of your inner dialogue are all wonderful tools for your personal evolution

The Great Key—The Place of Peaceful Poise

We are more than our minds and we are more than our feelings. We are manifestations of the energy of the Universe. This energy moves through us expanding as it experiences physical life. Our emotions guide us and inform us when we have lost touch with the truth of who we are and our life's purpose. The purpose of life is to experience and express joy. This journey to joy is accomplished through the expression of love, through our creativity, through compassion for others, through self-acceptance and through the knowledge that we are conduits for this amazing energy.

Our thoughts are powerful tools that can guide our emotions back into alignment with our true selves, that part of us that is connected to the Creative power of the Universe. The cycle of thoughts guiding emotions and emotions guiding us to greater openness, allowing more knowing, more creativity and more love to move through our physical bodies is the guidance of the universe to our soul, our higher self.

Throughout this book I have given you tools you can use to open your awareness and acceptance of this connection to guidance that is available to everyone.

In order to gain the greatest benefit from all of the tools you use in your journey to self—awareness and personal evolution, cultivate the practice of entering the place of peaceful poise.

Breathe, close your eyes, feel and appreciate the love of your own heart. Allow yourself to be in that moment, feeling joy, love and gratitude. It is in this place of peaceful poise that your greatest strength abides.

The development of this emotionally opened and balanced state brings you into alignment with your desires and gives the message to the Universe, through the emotion of joy, that you are open to all the love and blessings flowing to you and through you.

As you begin to know your own heart and accept its love, all things flow in an ever widening circle of love, prosperity, serenity and joy.

Meditations for the Bride and Groom, the CD by Rev Hannah Desmond (order form)

Hannah Desmond has created a CD to assist couples as they are planning their wedding and enjoying their married life.

HeartLight Meditations for the Bride and Groom contains two guided meditations.

The first meditation guides the bride into deep relaxation where stress is released and her emotions are soothed as she prepares herself for her wedding and her life. This twenty minute meditation is beneficial on all levels.

Heartlight Meditations CDs are available for purchase on Hannah's website at

http://www.heartlightweddings.info.

HEARTLIGHT MEDITATIONS FOR THE BRIDE AND GROOM

$10. When paid through PayPal shipping is free.

IN THE FLOW OF WELL BEING

$10. When paid through PayPal shipping is free.

The second guided meditation is for the bride and groom. Lying beside one another, they are gently guided through the 7 energy centers of the body. For example, as they are lead to the area of the throat, tension and blockages are released. As the attention is drawn to the heart, awareness of tightness, tension and emotional restrictions in the center of the chest may be felt. Suggestions are given to release energies that may block the flow of love, gratitude and prosperity.

The conscious release of energy blockages in the body brings awareness of the free flow of love, understanding and acceptance available.

The meditation ends as the couples' energy fields intermingle, strengthening the bridge of love and trust which exists between them. This twenty five minute meditation is a wonderful way to end the day and can be used through the years.